ECOLOGY

By

TERRY JENNINGS

WHAT IS ECOLOGY?

Nothing in the natural world lives entirely on its own. Every living thing, or *organism* (**ōr** • gə • ni • zəm), is affected by its surroundings. It is also affected by the other plants and animals around it. Environmental *factors* have an effect on animal and plant life. These factors include temperature, light, water, air, soil, and the weather. Living things also affect each other. The study of these relationships is called *ecology* (ē • **kä** • lə • jē). Ecologists try to find out how animals and plants fit into the world around them. The scientists also want to know how different organisms are connected to and work with other species.

INTERDEPENDENCE

Interdependence (in • tər • də • **pen** • dənts) means the way in which living organisms depend on each other in order to stay alive, grow, and breed. Bees, for example, depend on pollen and nectar from flowers for their food. Flowers, in turn, depend on bees to fertilize them so that they can produce seeds to make more flowering plants. Plants, in turn, produce oxygen gas, which all organisms need to live.

BIOMES

Ecologists divide the living world up into units called *biomes* (**bī** • ōmz). Biomes are shaped mainly by climate. They share the same types of plant life. Some of the main biomes include deserts, mountains, tropical rainforests, tropical grasslands, temperate forests, *coniferous* (kə • **ni** • fə • rəs) forests, and polar regions.

SCIENCE EXPLAINED: PRODUCTIVITY

Ecologists call the speed at which living things grow and breed productivity. Productivity is different in different places. Hot, dry areas such as the Sahara Desert are not very productive. Neither are the very cold regions of the Antarctic continent. The most productive ecosystems of all are tropical rainforests. The warm, wet conditions are perfect for the growth of plants. These plants provide food for huge numbers of animals.

ECOSYSTEMS

An *ecosystem* (ē • kō • sis • təm) is not just the plants and animals living in an area. In the case of a rainforest, it is made up of the trees, soil, air, water, minerals, and climate. It also includes the bacteria, *fungi* (**fung** • gī), plants, birds, insects, reptiles, and other organisms that live there. In a single ecosystem there may be hundreds or even thousands of species.

HABITATS

A *habitat* is any place where a group of organisms can live. Ponds, streams, rock pools, and prairies are all habitats. Large habitats, like forests, are made up of many smaller habitats. Each species of wild plant and animal has adapted to live in a particular habitat. Penguins, for example, are perfectly suited to their polar environment. They have flippers that allow them to swim through the water to catch fish. They also have thousands of tiny feathers and a layer of fat under their skin that allows them to handle the severe cold of the Antarctic.

BIODIVERSITY

All around the world, ecologists are naming and counting every kind of living organism. This helps us to understand the amazing variety of life on Earth. It also shows us how living things have changed over time. So far, ecologists have found and described more than 1.5 million different *species* (types of animals or plants). They include all kinds of plants and animals, fungi, bacteria, and other simple forms of life. No one knows the total number of species on Earth. It could be as many as 10 to 15 million. New species are discovered every week. This incredible variety of life is known as *biodiversity* (bī • ō • də • **vər** • si • tē).

SURVEYING VEGETATION

Ecologists spend a great deal of time mapping vegetation. *Vegetation*, or plant life, can change for natural reasons or because of human actions. Some areas, such as forests, deserts, and mountains, are very large or difficult to get to. Ecologists may use photography from an aircraft or a satellite to help them map these regions. Certain types of satellite photographs show different plants and vegetation in different colors, as in this image of Hawaii.

TRICKS & METHODS

To be good at their work, ecologists need to observe, measure, and record all the different parts of the area they are studying. They must count or map the different species of plants and animals. They also need to record where the organisms grow, their movements, and how they live, feed, and breed. Then they must measure the physical features of the environment. These features include soil moisture and acidity, temperature, wind speed, light intensity, and humidity. By comparing all these measurements and observations, ecologists can decide what conditions particular species need to survive. They also figure out what effects certain changes will have on the plants and animals in an ecosystem.

WATCHING WATER

Testing water for pollution is an important job for an ecologist. Sooner or later the water that we have used in our homes, schools, and factories finds its way into a river or the sea. This usually happens after it has been cleaned by a water treatment plant. But not all water is cleaned. *Polluted* (dirty) water is not always easy to spot. Ecologists regularly take samples of water from lakes, rivers, streams, and the sea. Back in the laboratory, they *analyze* (study) the water to see what chemicals it contains. Ecologists also regularly check on the wildlife living in the water. Any changes in wildlife population can mean the water is polluted.

FISHY BUSINESS

Ecologists sometimes tag fish they have weighed and measured in order to track the fish's movement and growth. If the fish is caught again later, they will know how far it has traveled and how much it has grown. Sometimes a tiny radio *transmitter* (**tranz** • mi • ter) is fitted under the skin of a fish, or fixed to its tail. The fish is returned to where it was first caught and tracked by a boat. The boat has a radio receiver that picks up signals from the transmitter attached to the fish. Sometimes similar transmitters are used to track birds and larger land animals.

FOOD DETECTIVES

It is important for an ecologist to know what foods wild animals eat. However, clues are not always easy to see. Ecologists have developed a *technique* (method) called fecal analysis to help them study an animal's diet. They collect the fresh droppings and put them into a preservative. Then, by examining tiny pieces under a microscope, they can see what the animal has been eating.

ALL CREATURES GREAT & SMALL

This ecologist is using a small trap called a Longworth trap. He wants to see how many mice, voles, snakes, and shrews are living in an area of woodland.

Some nesting material and food is placed in the box part of the trap. Then, when a small animal enters, it steps on a trip wire that shuts the door of the trap. The next day the animal can be identified, weighed, measured, and then released. Sometimes a large number of such traps are set in a line across an area of forest, swamp, or prairie. They give a clear picture of what kinds of small animals are living there.

PLANT LIFE ON EARTH

REMARKABLE RICE

Rice is a tropical grass cultivated by people. It provides the main cereal diet for half of the world's population in Asia and Central and South America. Rice is different from other cereals. It is usually grown in standing water in fields called paddy fields. The hollow rice stems allow oxygen down to the waterlogged roots of the plant. The flooded fields encourage the growth of tiny blue-green *algae* (**al** • jē). The algae are able to turn nitrogen from the air into fertilizer for the rice plant. The algae can make as much as 18 pounds (40 kilograms) of fertilizer for each acre of field.

There are more than 380,000 different species of plants in the world. They live in environments ranging from high mountains and desert plains to under the sea. In fact, wherever there is water, light, and reasonably warm conditions, plants are almost certain to grow. Plants are important to us because they help to make the air fit for us to breathe. Our food comes from plants, or from animals that eat plants. We also use plants in many other ways. We use them for building material and to make medicines, clothes, and perfumes. Even the paper used for this book came from plants.

PHOTOSYNTHESIS
(fō • tō • **sin** • thə • səs)

Green plants do not have to eat. They are the only living things that can make their own food from simple raw materials found in the air, water, and soil. They use carbon dioxide gas from the air and water from the soil. They get mineral salts from the water. The energy needed to join these materials together comes from sunlight.

Sunlight is trapped by a green substance called *chlorophyll* (**klōr** • ə • fil). Plants arrange their leaves to catch as much light as possible.

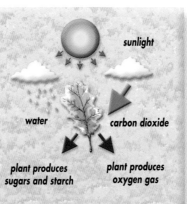

sunlight

water

carbon dioxide

plant produces sugars and starch

plant produces oxygen gas

ONE-HIT WONDERS

Sunflowers, like many other plants, live for only one growing season. They produce seeds and die. They belong to one of the largest families of flowering plants, with over 25,000 species. These include daisies, asters, ragwort, and dandelions. The plants of this family are unusual. What appears to be one flower is really a large number of small flowers. Sunflowers are grown for their seeds. The seeds are used to make cooking oil. Some of the oil is also used to make margarine, soaps, paints, and varnish. Sunflowers turn throughout the day so that they are always facing the sun.

SEEDS & CONES

Most of the larger plants we are familiar with grow from seeds. Most seeds come from flowers. A smaller number of plants have their seeds in cones. These include pine, larch, spruce, fir, and yew. They are often called conifers. Most conifers are large trees. The giant redwood trees of California (*right*) are enormous conifers. They grow to heights of more than 366 feet (110 meters). They are also the oldest living things on Earth. Redwoods can reach ages of up to 3,000 years. These giant trees grow in river valleys on the west coast of North America. Their vast size is partly due to the fertile soil and humid conditions of that region.

12,000ft	lichen
10,500ft	deep-rooted alpine flowers
9,000ft	low-growing shrubs
7,500ft	pasture
	conifers
6,000ft	
3,000ft	broad-leaved trees

ON THE LEVEL

Different plants can survive at different levels. On a mountain there is plenty of light for plants to grow. However, biting cold winds mean that only the toughest species can survive at high altitudes. On most tall mountains, broad-leaved trees such as beech and oak live on the lower slopes. Conifer trees live farther up the mountain. Above a certain height (the *tree-line*), it is too windy and cold for trees to be able to survive. The trees give way to tough grasses, mosses, lichens, and a few deep-rooted flowering plants.

SCIENCE EXPLAINED: STOMATA

Leaves have hundreds of tiny holes called stomata (stō • mə • tə). It is only possible to see stomata with a microscope. Carbon dioxide gas enters the leaves during the process called photosynthesis. This is the name given to the way in which green plants make their food. Oxygen gas produced as a waste gas goes out of the plant through these holes. All living things (including humans) need this oxygen to breathe. Water also evaporates from the plant through the stomata. A plant has to keep taking up water through its roots to avoid drying out.

Many snakes are too slow to chase their prey. Instead they hide and wait for a meal to pass. Different kinds of snakes kill their prey in different ways. Some snakes, such as this rock python from Africa (*right*), are called constrictors. They wrap themselves around their prey and squeeze hard. The prey soon runs out of breath and dies. Other snakes, such as adders and puff adders, poison their prey. They bite them with teeth called fangs that drip a poison (known as *venom*) into the wound. Snakes can open their jaws very wide and swallow their prey whole. A big meal such as this gazelle might last a python for several weeks.

THE ADAPTABLE AVOCET

Birds come in all shapes and sizes. Many live in specialized environments. The *avocet* (**a • və • set**) lives near seashores and salt marshes where it eats shrimp, ragworms, water snails, and other small invertebrates. In clear water the avocet pecks at its prey. In muddy water, where it cannot see clearly, it traps its food by feel. The bird holds its upturned bill slightly open under water, sweeping it from side to side. Unlike most wading birds, the avocet can swim well in deep water because it has partly webbed feet.

GRIZZLY FEAST

The brown or grizzly bear of Alaska, Canada, and the western United States is the largest of the seven species of bear in the world. Although brown bears have a reputation for being *ferocious* (fə • **rō** • shəs), they usually avoid humans. They spend much of their time alone. They wander around in search of food. Sometimes they find a lot to eat. Other times they go hungry. In summer and autumn there are fish, dead animals, and ripe fruits, nuts, and berries to eat. But for at least three months of the winter, the bears fast in their dens. During this time, the female brown bear also gives birth and nurses her young.

SCIENCE EXPLAINED: HERBIVORES VS CARNIVORES

All animals have to eat in order to survive. Their bodies are adapted to suit the kinds of food they eat. Animals that eat plants are called herbivores (ər • bə • vōrz). Larger herbivores have long, sharp front teeth that allow them to bite off pieces of plants. Their back teeth are flat and broad for grinding up tough vegetation. Animals that eat other animals are called carnivores (kär • nə • vōrz). The larger ones have sharp, pointed teeth and strong jaws for grabbing and slicing through flesh.

ANIMAL LIFE ON EARTH

Scientists like order and, if they can, they like to put things into groups. They group animals in a process called *classification* (klas • ə • fə • **kā** • shən). The animals with a backbone are called *vertebrates* (**vər** • tə • brəts). There are about 45,000 different vertebrates alive today. Animals without backbones are called *invertebrates*. They are an even larger and more varied group. Ninety-five percent of all the animals on Earth are invertebrates. Altogether there are about 950,000 different species ranging from single-celled animals to the giant squid. A giant squid may grow to be 66 feet (20 meters) long. Invertebrates can be found on land, in water, in the soil, in the air, and even in the snow of the polar ice caps.

LIFE IN THE OCEAN

Nearly three-quarters of the Earth is covered by water. Water habitats support many organisms. On the surface are floating animals and plants. Below the surface, a wealth of animal and plant life can be found. Corals, plants, fish, whales, and turtles all live under water. Even in the ocean, which goes down to incredible depths of over 36,000 feet (11,000 meters), life has found a way. There is no sunlight this far under water. These creatures get their energy from the Earth itself. Deep down in the ocean, huge sections of the seabed are constantly on the move. The movement produces hot water that gushes out of underwater vents. Bacteria feed on the chemicals released, and are in turn eaten by fish and other animals.

CLASSIFICATIONS

Ecologists put the thousands of different kinds of animals into groups to study. Each group contains animals that are alike in important ways. The first division is between vertebrates and invertebrates. Ecologists define many more types when organizing animals.

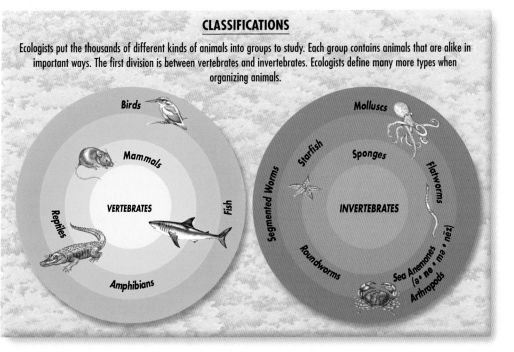

Birds

Mammals

Reptiles

VERTEBRATES

Fish

Amphibians

Molluscs

Segmented Worms

Starfish

Sponges

Flatworms

INVERTEBRATES

Roundworms

Sea Anemones (ə • **ne** • mə • nēz)

Arthropods

ECOSYSTEMS

Plants, animals, and the environment where they live form an *ecosystem*. An ecosystem can be as small as a pond or as large as an ocean. The whole ecosystem is powered by the sun. The sun provides the energy that lets green plants make their food. Apart from that, almost all the other food and energy supplies come from within the ecosystem. As well as plants, or their dead and decaying remains, all ecosystems contain animals.

Bear

Rabbit

Plants

Plants

FOOD CHAINS

The plants and animals in an ecosystem are linked together in food chains. Green plants make their own food, with the help of sunlight energy, so they start food chains. Animals cannot make their own food; they must get it elsewhere. Herbivorous animals eat plants, while carnivorous animals eat other animals. Sometimes a large carnivore will eat a smaller one. The arrows in a food chain mean "give food to." Usually as you go along a food chain the animals become larger but fewer in number.

Bobcat

Bear

Hawk

Rabbit

Shrew

Insects

Birds

Plants

Vole

Hawk

Bird

Insect

FOOD WEB

Ecosystems are made up of lots of different food chains. These chains are often linked to each other. Many kinds of herbivores feed on the same kinds of plants. Many carnivores prey on the same animals. Linked food chains from the same ecosystem are called *food webs*. Food webs help ecologists understand exactly how the plants and animals within an ecosystem depend on each other.

SCIENCE EXPLAINED: ENERGY & FOOD CHAINS

Plants and animals use food to produce energy. The energy helps them to grow, move, keep warm, and make seeds or have babies. At each step in a food chain, some energy is passed on. Most energy is lost in the form of heat. This means that there is much more energy at the beginning of a food chain than at the end. That is the reason why food chains rarely have more than four or five links. It is also the reason why no animal specializes in preying on large carnivores such as tigers, jaguars (jag • wôrz), or polar bears.

DECOMPOSERS AT WORK

P lants and animals are always multiplying. If they lived forever, the Earth would soon be overcrowded. Instead, all living things die after a while. But the surface of the Earth is not covered with thousands of dead plants and animals. This is because a group of living organisms specializes in feeding on dead plants and animals. They break them down into simple substances. Bacteria too small to be seen without a powerful microscope, fungi, worms, snails, fly maggots, and other small animals break down dead bodies and other waste materials. They turn them into smaller and smaller pieces. Finally, all the chemicals in them are released into the soil, water, or air. The chemicals can then be used to help other plants to grow.

Plants take root and the roots break up the log.

Woodlice live in the damp hole of rotten wood. In turn they are eaten by spiders

DELICIOUS DUNG

Despite our view of dung, some small animals, such as flies, beetles, and worms find it a wonderful source of food. The yellow dung flies (*above*) lay their eggs in any crack they can find in a new pile of dung. The larger and steamier the heap of dung, the more flies it attracts. The *larvae* (**lär • vī**), or baby insects, hatch from the eggs. Then they munch their way through the dung, safely removing it.

SCIENCE EXPLAINED: DETRITIVORES & DECOMPOSERS

Ecologists divided the living things that feed on dead animals and plants, dung, and other waste materials into two groups. Animals that feed on dead remains, such as beetles and flies (and their larvae or maggots), together with worms, millipedes, snails, slugs, and woodlice, are called detritivores (di • tri • tə • vōrz). They break the waste materials down into smaller and smaller pieces. It is then left to decomposers, such as bacteria and fungi, to finish the job. They completely break down dead plants and animals. This releases chemicals that other living things can use again.

Beetle larvae feed on wood.

CASE STUDY: A ROTTING LOG

A few fungi cause plant and animal diseases, but most decompose dead plants and animals and their wastes. In this picture, bracket fungi are growing on a fallen log. But you can only see a tiny part of each *fungus* (**fung** • gəs). This is the part that *reproduces*, or makes more of, the fungus by means of spores. Most of the fungus consists of a network of threads, called *hyphae* (**hī** • fē). These threads form a tangled web inside the tree trunk, slowly dissolving it away. Other decomposers include insects such as snails and slugs. They also eat large amounts of dead plant material. They chew on the plant fibers with a tooth-covered tongue called a *radula* (**ra** • jə • lə). The slugs and snails digest the *cellulose* (**sel** • yə • lōs), the main chemical in all plants. Their droppings then become available to fungi and bacteria to decompose away completely. Some species of slug are particularly fond of droppings and even eat dog dung. Finally, birds and reptiles, such as frogs, also join in the destruction. They chip away at the rotting log until it falls apart.

Springtails and other insects feed on dead leaves.

Bracket fungi hyphae slowly dissolve the log.

BODY BURIER

Sexton beetles are often called burying beetles. What they bury is the dead bodies of small animals. A number of these beetles will dig away the soil underneath a *corpse*, or dead body, to form a pit. The corpse falls into the pit. A pair of sexton beetles can bury a dead mouse in just a few minutes. They then lay their eggs in the dead flesh. The eggs hatch into larvae, or grubs, which feed on the corpse.

DEAD HUNGRY

Vultures eat only *carrion* (dead meat). They are wonderfully designed to survive by stealing and eating the dead bodies of animals. Soaring on their long, broad wings, the vultures' sharp eyesight allows them to spot a dead body from more than 1 mile (1.5 kilometers) away. These big, powerful birds then use their hooked beaks for stripping skin and flesh. Their heads and necks are usually bald. This is so no feathers are messed up when they are poking around in a corpse.

CHANGES IN NATURE

E cologists have discovered that many ecosystems change, often due to the seasons. There are also harder to see and slower changes. If, for example, a lawn is not mowed, it will soon be invaded by weeds that will grow up and choke the grass. The wind will blow the seeds of trees and flowers onto the weedy wasteland. Berry seeds from shrubs will be dropped by birds. Some of these seeds will grow. What was a lawn will become a patch of scrub. Small animals that like these conditions will move in. After a while the scrub will become woodland. These changes are called a *succession*. This is because different species (plant and animal) succeed each other.

SEASONAL CHANGES

In tropical areas, with temperatures constant year round, the amount of rainfall determines the season—dry or rainy. Farther north and south, there are four main seasons—spring, summer, autumn, and winter. These produce many changes in living things. Most broad-leaved trees lose all their leaves in the autumn and grow new ones in the spring. Some animals migrate to areas, often far away. They find conditions that are more suitable for feeding or breeding, or both. Other animals, like hedgehogs, bats, and snakes avoid the worst seasonal conditions by hibernating.

HELPFUL PONIES

In nature, the changes in a succession toward woodland may be held back by strong winds or very low temperatures. In some cases, repeated fires or grazing by rabbits and other animals can stop the succession at grassland. On some nature reserves, ecologists actually use grazing animals to stop an ecosystem from turning into woodland, as on this one in Norfolk, England. Shetland ponies eat any tree seedlings as they appear. Because the ponies eat the seedlings when they are small, the seedlings never grow into large trees. By keeping the trees from growing into a forest, the ponies stop the succession at a grassy vegetation ecosystem.

RETURNING HOME

The Shenandoah Valley in Virginia and West Virginia is a specially protected national park. It is home to bobcats (*above*), deer, ravens, owls, and a host of other animals. These animals all form part of the food web. But it hasn't always been like that. During the 19th century there was hardly a tree in sight. Instead, there were farmhouses, cows, pigs, and fields of cabbages. Early settlers had cleared all the trees and farmed the land. The crops started to fail at the beginning of the 20th century. At that time, the government decided to abandon the land to nature. Within 20 years the first trees had appeared. Now it is one of the wildest places in North America.

Grazing animals eat the vegetation.

The sands of the desert creep forward as there is no vegetation to stop it.

Farmers eventually move as the land becomes barren.

Farming land exposes the topsoil to the sun.

DESERTIFICATION

As man continues to have an ever greater effect on the planet, the world's deserts continue to grow. By chopping down trees and grazing too many animals on scrub and grassland, people have left soil open to the weather. The sun, wind, and rain dry out the topsoil. The topsoil is then blown and washed away, leaving a desert. Overfarming land can also cause *desertification*. As the soil is overworked, a desert wasteland is created. This happened in the American prairies in the 1930s, when a huge area of barren land called the Dust Bowl was created.

SCIENCE EXPLAINED: NATURAL SELECTION

A famous 19th-century scientist, Charles Darwin, studied how animals and plants became so well-adapted to their way of life. Darwin concluded that individual plants and animals sometimes have features that help them to survive. On a lettuce plant, for example, a green bug would probably survive longer than a brown bug. This is because the green bug would be harder to see and less likely to be eaten. The green bugs that live the longest are likely to have more babies and pass on their color. Over a long period of time, each species will gradually develop the most useful features for surviving in its own environment. Darwin called this process natural selection.

WONDERFUL WEEDS

Some of the most adaptable plants are the ones we call "weeds." A weed is simply a plant growing where we don't want it to. Weeds can grow and spread on almost any piece of bare or neglected ground. They can flower and produce seeds at almost any time of the year. Some of the most adaptable don't even need to produce seeds. If one tiny part of the root is broken off or left in the soil, it will grow into a new plant.

KNOCK ON WOOD

It would be hard to think of a bird better designed for living in trees than a woodpecker. Woodpeckers feed on wood-boring insects and grubs. Their large feet have two toes pointing forward and two backward for gripping tree trunks. The woodpecker's stiff tail feathers are used to support its weight. Its strong beak is the perfect tool for hammering, drilling, and chiseling wood. It also has special shock-absorbers in its head that prevent headaches! Once the woodpecker has found an insect or grub, it uses its long, sticky tongue to grab the tasty food.

ADAPTATION

We are often amazed at how well plants and animals are suited, or adapted, to their environment. The polar bear's white coat allows it to hunt almost unseen in the snowy wastes of the Arctic. The tiny hummingbird is able to suck nectar from tropical flowers because of its long beak and marvelous ability to hover in the air. Some ecosystems are perfect for one type of animal or plant and very dangerous for another. On the other hand, some plants and animals are very adaptable and can quickly make a home more or less anywhere.

DESERT FOX

The fennec fox lives in the Sahara and Arabian deserts. Its color matches the desert sands. Its large ears give off heat and help the fox to keep cool. The large ears also give the fennec fox very good hearing. It uses its ears to locate gerbils, lizards, insects, and other prey at a distance. It spends the daytime resting in its cool den. The fennec comes out to hunt only at night when the air is cooler. Then its large eyes help it to see in the dark.

ORCHID ATTRACTION

The bee orchid is a master of disguise. The flower of this remarkable plant seems to have a bee resting on it. The "body" of the "bee" even feels furry. It gives off a scent exactly like that produced by a female bee. This fools male bees who fly in to "mate" with the flower. In doing so, they become covered with pollen. The bee may then carry the pollen to another flower of the same kind. This pollination will allow the flower to produce seeds.

CITY LIVING

Living in a city has certain advantages over living in the country for wildlife. The heat produced by people and buildings makes the city a warm place to live in. Buildings provide shelter from the wind and safe places to breed. Food is plentiful in the city's garbage cans. Raccoons have successfully adapted to life in many North American cities. At night they search the garbage cans and, if they can, cupboards and refrigerators. Some have even discovered how to open corked bottles to drink the contents.

COMPETITION

All living things reproduce. Usually they have far more babies than can possibly survive. For example, a large female cod can lay 10 million eggs at once. If all the cod eggs hatched and grew into adult fish there would not be enough food for them in the sea. What really happens is what ecologists call a struggle for survival, or *competition*. Living things have to compete for space, nesting sites, food, and all the other things they need to survive. Only the fittest and best adapted individuals survive.

SURVIVING THE COMPETITION

Dandelions are one of the most successful and common weeds. Their feathery fruits each contain a single seed. The seeds are spread by the wind. Once established, their deep and tough roots help them to survive most efforts to remove them. Even a small piece of root left in the ground can grow into a whole new plant within a few weeks. What dandelions cannot compete with is taller and longer-living plants, such as shrubs and trees. These plants eventually overshadow and kill them.

FIGHTING FOR SPACE

In September, birch trees produce thousands of winged seeds that are scattered by the wind. They take root in forest clearings and areas that have recently been burnt. The following spring, a mass of tiny seedlings appear. Many are eaten by slugs, millipedes, woodlice, rabbits, and other herbivores. Even more of the seedlings die because they are unable to compete with faster-growing plants. Even if the birch seedlings grow into adult trees, they rarely become really large because they are overshadowed by taller trees.

FIGHTING FOR FOOD

Cheetahs are successful hunters, but they are surrounded by would-be food thieves. With its slim, streamlined body and long legs, the cheetah can accelerate from a standstill to 60 mph (100 km/h) in three seconds—faster than any sports car. It can reach a top speed of 70 mph (115 km/h). Once it has caught its prey, the cheetah must rest and cool off before it can eat. During that time it faces competition for its food from lions, hyenas, jackals, and even vultures. As a result, cheetahs lose a lot of their prey.

MOTHERS' MEETING

Like seabirds, seals spend most of their lives at sea, meeting on land only to breed and *molt* (shed its old coat). By coming ashore, the seals are guaranteed to meet others of the same species for mating. When the seals do come ashore on some lonely beach, they have to compete with each other for mates. They also have to compete for a space where they can rest and nurse their young.

SCIENCE EXPLAINED: THE HUMAN FACTOR

One major kind of competition that all wild plants and animals have to face is from the rapidly growing human population. As the population grows, more of the wild places where plants and animals live are being destroyed. Hedges, woods, and forests are being cut down to make fields. Ponds and marshes are drained for farmland or for building. Roads are built on prairies and houses are built on meadows. Pollution from human activities destroys wildlife homes everywhere.

HABITATS & NICHES

A *habitat* is a place where a plant or animal lives. Some species are found in several habitats, while others are more specialized and can only survive in one habitat. Giant pandas, for example, can only live in the bamboo forests of central China. They have become endangered because large areas of this particular habitat have been cut down. Within an ecosystem there can be many different habitats. Each species has to find a habitat where it can easily obtain food. It also needs the levels of water, light, and heat that suit its way of life. This is called its *niche* (nich). Because different species tend to have different niches, they avoid competing with each other.

FINDING A NICHE

The *gerenuk* (gā • rə • nük) is a kind of gazelle that has found its own special niche in the grasslands and scrub of East Africa. Gerenuks feed on the leaves of the *acacia* (ə • kā • shə) tree, as do impala and giraffes. But the impala stands on all fours to eat the acacia leaves, while the giraffe's long neck allows it to reach the leaves up to 20 feet (6 meters) off the ground. The gerenuk has a long neck, and, in order to feed, it stands on its hind legs. Its forefeet touch the bush or tree. It can therefore eat the acacia leaves that are too high for impala to reach and too low for giraffes.

THE HIGH LIFE

The koala of eastern Australia has a very specialized niche as a tree-dweller. It lives in eucalyptus forests and rarely comes to the ground. On the ground it would be easy prey for dingoes, cats, and dogs. Since it has little opportunity for drinking, the koala gets its moisture from the leathery eucalyptus leaves. It eats about 2.2 pounds (1 kilogram) of these each night. Then it saves energy by sleeping for up to 18 hours each day—in a eucalyptus tree, of course!

UNFUSSY FEEDERS

Some animals are not fussy about what they eat or where they live. The red fox was once confined to wooded country areas where it was hunted because it killed farm and game birds. It was always an adaptable feeder and in recent years the fox has moved into towns and cities. In these areas it takes advantage of the cover, lack of hunters, and large amount of food available. Many foxes now live in gardens, wastelands, and near railroad tracks. They scavenge on garbage.

greenfinch

bullfinch

crossbill

FINCHES

These three closely related species of finch do not compete because each has become adapted to different foods. The greenfinch has a strong pointed beak. It uses its beak to pick open and crack seeds and cereal grains. The bullfinch uses its short strong beak to eat the seeds of ash, birch, nettle dock, and berries. When food is scarce, it turns to the buds of fruit trees and flowering shrubs. The crossbill uses its strange crossed-over beak to reach the seeds from the cones of pines and other conifer trees.

SCIENCE EXPLAINED: A NICHE WITHIN A NICHE

*Species that live in a habitat where food can be scarce often have niches that prevent them from competing with each other. The cormorant (**kôr • mə • rant**) and the shag, for example, are birds that live along the coast and dive for fish. But the cormorant dives deeper, while the shag concentrates on the fish closer to the surface. Similarly, grey seals and common seals avoid competition for scarce breeding sites. This is because common seals tend to breed on sandy beaches and sandbanks during June and July. Grey seals mostly breed on rocky coasts and in caves in the autumn and early winter.*

POPULATIONS: IN DANGER

As a result of human activities it is estimated that one-fifth of all species are in danger of *extinction*. Some animals are hunted for their tusks, skins, and meat. Others are taken from the wild and sold to collectors. But the biggest single reason why plants and animals are endangered is because habitats are being destroyed or polluted.

THE BLUE WHALE

The blue whale is the largest animal that has ever lived. It can grow to be over 100 feet (30 meters) long and can weigh more than 150 tons (136,000 kilograms). That is about as heavy as 25 fully-grown African elephants.

In spite of its vast size, a blue whale feeds on tiny plankton. Blue whales were hunted so much in the past for their meat and fat (which was made into oil) that they nearly became extinct. It is believed that there are less than 10,000 blue whales left today.

THE RHINOCEROS

There are five species of rhinoceros in the world. All are on the verge of extinction because *poachers* (illegal hunters) kill them to sell their horns. These are used to make medicines that some people believe will cure headaches, fevers, and other illnesses. Rhino horns are also sold to make dagger handles. In some game reserves in Africa, people are trying to protect rhinoceroses by sawing off their horns. If they don't have horns, the poachers leave them alone.

RAFFLESIA

At up to 3 feet (90 cm) across and weighing about 15 pounds (7 kilograms), the *rafflesia* (rə • **flē** • zhē • ə) plant has the largest flower in the world. It is also the smelliest and one of the most endangered. The rafflesia is a plant *parasite* (**pā** • rə • sīt). This means it depends on other plants to survive. It has no leaves and takes its water and sugar from the roots of other rainforest plants. The flower is covered in warts and produces a smell like rotting meat to attract the flies it uses for pollination. It is sometimes referred to as the "corpse lily." Destruction of the tropical rainforest in Southeast Asia has severely reduced its habitat.

POPULATIONS: NATURAL CONTROL

Every living thing can reproduce, some at an alarming rate. A simple *bacterium* (bak • tē • rē • um), for example, can split into two every 20 minutes. If there was nothing to stop their growth, after 36 hours a layer of bacteria 1 foot (30 cm) deep would cover the entire surface of the Earth. Fortunately these incredible increases in population do not happen. Natural checks such as shortages of food and space, unsuitable temperatures, disease, and other factors keep populations under control.

HOUSEFLIES

Houseflies lay their eggs in trash cans, stale food, corpses, and dung. If all of the offspring of one pair of houseflies survived and bred, they would be able to cover the entire surface of the Earth to a depth of 47 feet (14 meters) in a single summer. Fortunately cold, wet weather, disease, predators, such as spiders and birds, and people with fly swatters or chemical *insecticides* (in • sek • tə • sīdz), all help to keep the number of flies at a reasonable level.

BROWN RATS

Some towns and cities contain more rats than people. Rats cause damage and spread disease. They also breed rapidly from a young age. One ecologist calculated that a pair of rats could possibly produce 20 million descendants in three years. Fortunately, rats die of disease or starvation. They may not be able to find a mate or a warm, dry nesting site. Many are eaten by owls, hawks, foxes, and other enemies. Even more are trapped or poisoned by people.

CASE STUDY: THE GALAPAGOS OIL DISASTER

The *Galapagos* (gə • **la** • pə • gōs) Islands are a group of 13 major islands and more than 115 smaller ones that lie about 600 miles (960 km) off the coast of South America. In 1885 they were visited by Charles Darwin, inspiring his theory of evolution. Today, the Galapagos Islands are still home to a large population of plants and animals. Many of these organisms are found nowhere else on Earth. In January 2001, this unique group of wildlife was threatened when an oil tanker ran aground. Quick work by ecologists helped to avoid a major environmental disaster.

PREVENTIVE MEASURES

Immediately after the tanker crashed, floating barriers (or booms) were put up around the *Jessica*. These booms are like a row of rubber hot dogs floating on the water. They are designed to stop the oil spreading out across the surface. The scientists also put layers of absorbent material on the surface of the sea around the ship to soak up any leaking oil. When the oil spread out beyond the booms and *absorbent* (əb • **zōr** • bənt) materials, it was sprayed with chemicals to break it down. At the same time, experts began trying to safely pump the remaining oil out of the tanker.

OIL & WILDLIFE

Oil destroys the waterproofing on the fur of mammals and the feathers of birds. This causes them to die of cold unless quickly rescued. So when the tanker crashed, ecologists from the Galapagos research station carried out a quick survey of the wildlife populations likely to be affected by the oil. This included seabirds, which would be unable to fly if they became covered in oil. Also, the birds would be poisoned if they attempted to clean themselves. Invertebrate animals were also at risk. They feed by sifting food particles from the water. Both invertebrates and fish breathe with gills. Oil can coat these delicate *mechanisms* (**me** • kə • ni • zəmz), quickly killing the animal.

SCIENCE EXPLAINED: SPILT OIL

Most kinds of oil float on seawater. The oil usually spreads out rapidly across the surface of the water. It forms a layer we call an oil slick. As the oil spreads further and further, it forms a thinner and thinner layer. Eventually it makes a very thin, rainbow-colored layer called a sheen. In the end, the oil may evaporate or form tar balls that sink and are slowly broken down by bacteria in the sea. Often this happens only after the oil has caused a great deal of damage to wildlife and the environment.

THE DAMAGE

Amazingly, only about 30 sea lions and 5 sea birds had to be cleaned of the oil. Although most of the ship's cargo leaked out, it did not do too much damage. Fortunately, the hot sun evaporated a lot of the oil. The winds and ocean currents carried much of the rest away from the islands. All the sea cucumbers, sea urchins, and many other invertebrate animals, fish, and seaweeds in the area of the *Jessica* were killed. Mercifully, the larger animals were much luckier.

THE FUTURE

The Galapagos Islands are home to giant *tortoises* (tōr • tə • səz) that live nowhere else in the world. Ecologists from the Charles Darwin Foundation on San Cristobal and from the World Wildlife Fund will be making regular checks on these and all other Galapagos species for several years. They will pay close attention to sensitive indicator species, such as algae, sea urchins, sea cucumbers, marine iguanas, sea lions, and lava gulls. Any reduction in the numbers of one species could easily have a disastrous effect on other species.

ALIEN INVADERS

Humans have been responsible for introducing alien species to new regions, sometimes accidentally and sometimes on purpose. Often these alien plants and animals spread out of control and destroy native wildlife. The best-known species to be accidentally spread is the brown rat. It originated in Asia and spread throughout the world to become a pest to people and their crops, a carrier of disease, and a predator. It has helped to make extinct at least nine species of flightless birds in New Zealand. Species introduced on purpose include dogs, cats, rabbits, squirrels, various birds, and most other domestic animals.

A REAL CHOKER

In 1884, some water *hyacinths* (hī • ə • sinths) from Brazil were taken to a gardening exhibition in New Orleans in Louisiana. A few gardeners took pieces home to plant in their garden ponds. Soon, the plants grew too big for the garden ponds. The gardeners threw the unwanted pieces into nearby streams. Within 90 years, the water hyacinth had spread across much of the southern United States, Australia, India, South Africa, and Malaysia. Rivers and lakes were choked with a mat of this plant, 39 inches (1 meter) thick. The plants blocked out sunlight from the water. The water quickly lost oxygen and more wildlife died.

CULLING THE NUTRIA

A native of South America, the *nutria* (nū • trē • ə), also known as the coypu, was introduced into Britain, other European countries, the United States, and parts of Africa to be farmed for its fur. Some of these giant rat-like animals, each weighing up to 15 pounds (7 kilograms), escaped and became pests. They damaged crops and natural vegetation. They also harmed the river banks in which they made their burrows. With few natural enemies, the populations of nutria thrived. After intensive trapping and shooting they were finally removed from Britain in the 1980s. They remain a pest elsewhere, including the United States.

GREEDY GOAT

Among the most destructive of the introduced animals are goats. In the 19th century, sailors introduced goats to the Galapagos Islands to kill for meat at a later date. However, the goats destroyed the habitat of the giant tortoises by eating up all the vegetation. Rats (also introduced by accident) ate the turtles' young. Today the tortoises are protected by law and have to be bred in captivity on the islands.

RABBITS RUNNING RIOT

Rabbits came originally from North Africa and the countries around the Mediterranean Sea. They were introduced to other countries, including the British Isles, New Zealand, Australia, and Chile, to be farmed for their meat. They escaped and bred—like rabbits—destroying crops and young trees. The rabbit shook off predators, such as dogs, cats, foxes, stoats, and weasels. It was unaffected by human attack with gas, gun, trap, and snare. The rabbit populations were eventually brought under control when a virus disease, called *myxomatosis* (mik • sō • mə • tō • sis), killed millions of them.

SCIENCE EXPLAINED: DISRUPTING FOOD CHAINS

*People have been introducing new plants and animals into different parts of the world for hundreds of years. Nearly all our cereals, wheat, oats, and barley originally came from Asia Minor. Our cattle came from Asia and our chickens from the East. For the most part, these plants and animals were under our control. It is a different matter when plants and animals are set free and left to their own devices. They become a nuisance (**nū** • sents) because in their new environments there are often no natural predators to control their numbers.*

MONGOOSE MISCHIEF

In their native homelands, which stretch from Iraq to India and south to Malaysia, mongooses feed on pest animals, including rats, mice, snakes, scorpions, centipedes, and wasps. Mongooses were introduced into the West Indies to destroy the rats and snakes that were invading the sugar cane and other crops. Instead, the mongooses turned to eating the more easily caught native species. They allowed the rats and snakes to thrive. *Solenodons* (sō • **lē** • nə • dänz), insect-eating animals found only in Cuba, Haiti, and the Dominican Republic, are now threatened with extinction by the mongooses.

FAMINE VICTIMS

If too many animals have to survive in one place they may destroy the vegetation that is keeping them alive. This has happened in the areas around the Sahara Desert. The number of people and domestic animals has increased. The grass has been eaten and trampled on by goats, sheep, and other animals so that there is little vegetation left. When it does rain, the water runs off the surface of the land before it has time to sink into the soil. The land turns into desert while the people starve to death unless they receive food aid.

LIVING IN HARMONY

The early human beings were hunter-gatherers. They lived in peace with their environment. They wandered across the countryside collecting leaves, wild fruits, nuts, and seeds to eat. They killed the occasional animal to add to their diet. Early humans had little effect on their environment since there were not many of them. They were also constantly moving in search of new sources of food. Some tribal people in South America, Africa, Asia, and Australia still live like this. However, most people now live a settled life, mostly in towns and cities. They have a huge effect on the environment in which they live.

HUMAN ECOLOGY & IMPACT

Two-thirds of the Earth's surface is covered by oceans and seas. Much of the remaining land is made up of mountains, deserts, and polar regions—places that are difficult for people to live in. People need food, homes, clothes, fuels, and other materials. These come directly or indirectly from the land. Today the land is under pressure from an ever-increasing human population. In 1650 the world population was only 500 million; today there are more than 6.7 billion of us on Earth. More people means more pollution, *desertification* (di • zər • tə • fə • **kā** • shən), and destruction of wildlife and wildlife habitats.

LADYBUGS & APHIDS

The small, brightly-colored ladybug is the most familiar of beetles and also one of the most helpful to farmers and gardeners. The adult beetles and their grubs feed mostly on aphids and are important in keeping these insect pests in check. A fully-grown grub can eat about 50 aphids a day. Nowadays some gardeners and farmers are actually introducing ladybugs to their crops to allow them to control aphids and other insect pests. This is called biological control.

POWER STATION
Power stations and factories pollute the air, producing acid rain and causing global warming. They also pollute rivers, lakes, and the sea.

BUILDING WORK
As the human population continues to increase, more and more houses are being built on previously undisturbed sites.

MOTOR VEHICLES
As well as causing noise, cars and trucks produce exhaust fumes which add to acid rain and global warming.

SPRAYING PESTICIDES
Farmers often spray their crops with pesticides (pes • tə • sīdz) and fertilizers. These may harm wildlife and also make human food and drinking water unsafe.

A LOAD OF GARBAGE
Garbage is ugly and poses a danger to people and wildlife. It is also a waste of valuable resources, since much of it could be recycled.

STUDYING PLANT LIFE IN A TROPICAL RAINFOREST

If we are to understand and save the remaining rainforests, we have to know what lives there. This is not easy when many of the animals feed high in the trees. These trees are often 100 feet (30 meters) tall. Ecologists now have to use some of the equipment of rock-climbers, including climbing irons, ropes, and harnesses, to get close to the plants and animals high in the tree canopy. Often they build walkways from the top of one tree to the next.

ECOLOGISTS & ECOLOGY TODAY

The German biologist Ernst Haeckel first used the word "oecology" in 1866 to describe the study of living things and the way they interacted with the world around them. The modern spelling of ecology was not used until 1893. Since those days, ecology has progressed from the recording and describing of living things in their natural surroundings to a complex study. Modern ecologists use science, mathematics, computer science, and statistics to provide detailed and accurate measurements about the environment and the living things in it. Today, ecology and ecologists are more necessary than ever. They predict and measure the impact of human activities on the environment.

REINTRODUCING ANIMALS

The sea eagle is a magnificent bird of prey that became extinct in the British Isles in 1916. Ecologists studied the birds' habitat and life history for many years. In 1975, British ecologists released imported sea eagle chicks on an island off the west coast of Scotland. After a very slow start, the birds began to nest and breed. Then they spread out to other parts of Scotland. By 2000 there were 23 pairs of sea eagles in western Scotland and the total number of chicks reared by them had reached 100.

ECOLOGISTS IN ANTARCTICA

The polar regions are the last true wilderness left on Earth. Even here changes to the environment are taking place. Pipelines now carry oil and gas across the frozen land of the Arctic. Increasing numbers of cruise ships take tourists to Antarctica. Ecologists are busy studying the effects of these changes. In Antarctica ecologists from many countries work side by side to study penguins, seals, whales, and other wildlife on that continent.

RECORDING FISH LIFE

Although ecologists now use many modern electronic and scientific devices, much of their work still involves careful observation on land and under water. These ecologists are measuring and examining pike from a local lake. Their results will be fed into a computer and analyzed when they get back to the laboratory. Such analysis will save hundreds of hours of complicated calculations.

CULTURING RARE PLANTS

Some plants are extremely rare and attempts are being made to grow them in the laboratory so that eventually they can be returned to the wild. Many rare plants are difficult to grow from seeds. Ecologists have developed a way of producing new plants from a tiny fragment in a test-tube containing a special jelly. This technique works well with some rare *orchids* (ōr • kidz) and it means that many new plants can be grown from just one parent.

SCIENCE EXPLAINED: BOMB CALORIMETERS

One of the most important techniques now used by ecologists involves measuring the amount of energy passing along the various food chains in an ecosystem. To take their measurements, they use an instrument called a bomb calorimeter (ka • lə • ri • mə • tər). A sample of plant or animal material is put inside the "bomb" of the calorimeter. The calorimeter is then sealed up. The piece of plant or animal is burnt and the increase in temperature is measured. This is converted to an energy measurement in joules (jūlz) or kilojoules. Because of such studies we now know that only about 10 percent of energy is passed from one link in a food chain to the next.

GLOSSARY

Biodiversity—The variety of life on Earth

Biological control—The use of natural predators instead of chemicals to control other species

Biomes—Areas of the world characterized by their climate and plant life

Boom—A floating barrier used to prevent oil spreading out after a large spill

Canopy—The top layer of a tropical rainforest

Carnivore—An animal that eats other animals

Classification—The process by which ecologists sort animals with similar characteristics into groups

Culturing—The growing of plants in the laboratory from pieces of a parent plant

Decomposer—An animal that completely breaks down dead plants and animals, releasing chemicals that other living things can use again

Detrivores—An animal that feeds on dead remains, breaking them down into smaller pieces

Ecosystem—The interaction between plants, animals and the environment in which they live

Exhaustion—The overworking of a habitat until it can no longer sustain any life

Habitat—A place where a group of organisms live

Herbivore—A plant-eating animal

Invertebrate—An animal without a backbone

Niche—A highly specialized habitat within an ecosystem

Predator—An animal or plant that preys on other animals

Productivity—The rate at which living things grow and breed

Photosynthesis—The method by which plants use sunlight to get their energy from water and carbon dioxide

Sensitive indicator species—Delicate species ecologists monitor to study the condition of a habitat

Stomata—Tiny holes in plant leaves that let carbon dioxide in and oxygen and water out

Succession—A change in nature where one set of plant and animal species disappear from a habitat and are succeeded by another

Vertebrate—An animal with a backbone

First published in Great Britain by ticktock Publishing Ltd. Printed in China.

ISBN-13: 978-1-59905-444-5   ISBN-10: 1-59905-444-2   eBook: 978-1-60291-770-5

15 14 13 12 11 1 2 3 4 5

Picture Credits:
t=top, b=botto c=center, l=left, r=right, OFC=outside front cover, IFC=inside front cover, IBC=inside back cover, OBC=outside back cover

ATG: 4t. Ardea: 19c, 22–23s, 23b. Bruce Coleman Collection: 6tl, 8t, 12tl, 12–13c, 14b, 16b, 17tr, 20l, 22tl, 22b & OBC. Corbis Images: 14–15c, 17c, 24t, 24cl, 24–25c, 25tr & OBC, 25cr, 26–27b, 27b, 28t, 28c, 30cl, 31t, 31c. Ecoscene: 19t. Environmental Images: 6–7c, 16t, 26t. The Environmental Picture Library: 7r, 18b. FLPA: 3t, 8b, 21t, 24b, 27tl. Terry Jennings: 2c, 14c, 18t. Oxford Scientific Films: 2tl, 2b. Science Photo Library: OFC. Still Pictures: 3b, 9c, 17br.

Every effort has been made to trace the copyright holders and we apologize in advance for any unintentional omissions.
We would be pleased to insert the appropriate acknowledgement in any subsequent edition of this publication.

SADDLEBACK
EDUCATIONAL PUBLISHING